Pieces of a Reluctant Memoir
Michelle Golden

Copyright © 2020 Michelle Golden

All rights reserved. No part of this book may be reproduced or transmitted in any form or by any means, electronic or mechanical, including photocopying, recording or by any information storage and retrieval system without permission in writing from the publisher.

The Bee's Knees Publications – Mount Horeb, WI
ISBN: 978-0-578-69216-6
Library of Congress Control Number: 2020908705
Title: *Pieces of a Reluctant Memoir*
Author: Michelle Golden
Digital distribution | 2020
Paperback | 2020

Cover Photo Credit: Jeff Golden, "Reflections of Last Year"

This is a work of fiction. The characters, names, incidents, places, and dialogue are products of the author's imagination, and are not to be construed as real.

Dedication

For my husband Jeffrey and children Samuel, Emelia, and Eleanor. You are my greatest life's work.

Table of Contents

Part One: The Love
A Sunbath for the Leaves 2
Slicing the Moon 3
Shh 5
Feet Planted 6
A Love Song 8
Remember Babylon 9
Numbers and Situations 10

Part Two: The Break
Superficial Bookmarks 14
It May be Used 15
Look up at your World 16
Hopes and Dreams Begin and End Here 17
Shoot 18
Better than Before 19
Call me Crazy 20

Part Three: The Fall
Mischievous Misgivings 22
Store this Soul in a Cool Dry Place 23
Swaying Elegantly in my Seat 24
Miles Left Sleeping 25
Ready. Set. Gone 26
Reduce. Reuse. Recycle 27
Something Small 28

Part Four: The Search
Incessant Gardening 30
Life's Lament 31
"He" is a pronoun. It Replaces What's Real 32
Pretty and Predictable 33
Pieces of a Reluctant Memoir 34
Solitude 36
Unusual Donation 37

Part Five: The Light
Tread Lightly.. 40
Walk with an Umbrella.. 41
Breath Taking.. 43
Between the Lines.. 44
Hollow Stranger 45
Sangria.. 46
Meditation 47

Part One: The Love

Love is a bit of a stranglehold
Where you can't give up and you can't let go.
I'm waiting for the shade to wash over
And cool me with its dark emptiness.
A temporary shield-
Given only by my place in line.

Pieces of a Reluctant Memoir

A Sunbath for the Leaves

White-washed and linen-free
I'd open up my arms for thee.
I'd unlock all doubt and set it loose-
Trip in my own planted noose.
Finish the blackboard's secret phrase.
O, what a petty waste of days.
I'm trapped under the helm of fear
Waiting for my own ghosts to appear.
Chalet concealed in the mountain air,
I'd quit my life to take you there.
But I shouldn't speak of things thus far.
I'll have to subterfuge to avoid this mar.

Blossoming forth into the cool dusk and porch-lit
Facades.

The Love

Slicing the Moon

Love, for all of its wonder
Is taking me whole and
Then holding me under
Waves of pure insanity.
Thoughts meander,
Spent at last by the vast
Men of constant banter.
Escaping out of the palm,
Trying to keep it in.
Never reacting-
Always overreacting.
Becoming someone
I don't even think I see.
Looking through tough pages,
Ripped and torn for ages.
Let me in-let me read-
For your mind is a budding seed;
I can't get enough.
There are no more advances,
Just touches and glances.
Me, I am possessed by a fire
That engulfs all of your wishes-
Don't worry, I will take care.
Close all the windows; lock out the air.
I'm more or less somebody sleeping,
Shutting your eyes and bringing you with me.
Whispering all my defenses
Fearing the past tenses
Forgetting that I'd sink in your senses.
(If you let me that close to your soul)

Pieces of a Reluctant Memoir

The afternoon is ever-grey
While shards of sun come out to say,
"Anyone who is living
should come out and bear witness."

Love, and all of its glory and wonder
Is wrapped up in my sheets.
Sometimes that's where he sleeps.
Maybe if I keep the curtains drawn,
He might stay a little longer.
For then will my love grow fonder.

The Love

Shh...

I am enthralled in your mind.
Sucked into your senses,
You're one of a kind.

How I'd kill to be young and refined.
Pulled into your anguish,
My soul's what you'll find.

For Love, our paths have entwined.
We'd travel existence
With our thoughts we'd enshrine.

Just take me, my heart you have mined.
It's fair if you're Justice
Unless you're mankind.

I am nothing but blind.
Entranced by your wisdom
You're only divine.

Pieces of a Reluctant Memoir

Feet Planted

I'm covering the roads from living to defrosting
And I'm taken aback by the wrongs of the lives
Of the people who sing and ignore their night's dreams-
Deep into the emptiness of longing and sorrow.
For all misinterpretations are meant for morning hours.
(Only then does this thinking begin like a bitter infection)
Well, I'm being too tempestuous-
Sinking in the waters of your glorious eyes;
A well of prosperity in things much bigger than me.

Evenings that remind me of times of earnest love
And those easy days that close into an envelope of stars.
Wishing on the scenic route for something more than sane;
Yet, I'm the sort of fool who *feels* she can *feel* it
But if I were sailing on a wild wind, I can't say that I'd know
Just how to unravel my kite strings and learn to let go.
The kids are behaving the way that we used to.
Alas, I see the door of opportunity beginning to close.
Looking down at the time on my hand, (none to spare)
I find the sunny days I once thought crippled my complexion
Are no longer mine to spare.

Just blossom with me under the cool of a tree
With the light through the leaves brightening your eyes-
Those fountains of youth that I cannot deny.
Ten thousand songs couldn't make sense of this feeling.
So I revel in you in almost every way possible.
I'm into you so deep that I forget that I'm living.
I forget how to do anything but just hold you closer.

The Love

For you melt off the icy shell that has encompassed my soul
(So it's when you free me that I'm defrosting)
And while it feels as though I'll never again feel my toes,
And my hands sleep so long they go into hibernation,
Warming up next to you is the sweetest liberation.

Pieces of a Reluctant Memoir

A Love Song

If there was a world
Where you could be mine
I'd give up the stars
And I'd give up the skies.
I'd leave behind
All that I once knew
Only to live
In a world with just you.

If there was a love
Deeper than the sea
I'd drown in its wonders
So you could love me.
I'd leave the earth
And all I once knew
Only to live
In a world with just you.

Don't tell me I'm crazy
Because I'm crazy for you.
You give me a feeling
That my heart is brand new.
Your eyes tell me one thing
Your lips say much more
And I'd give up forever
To be the one you adore.

If there was a place
Or a moment or two
Where I could just stay
And fall more in love with you;
I'd suspend time
Give up all I once knew
Only to live
In a world with just you.

The Love

Remember Babylon

Take my faults, my words, my soul,
Take anything that makes you whole.
Take my belongings, body and heart,
Take this creation and take it apart.
Take my sight, my voice my hearing,
Take what I'm craving, what I'm fearing.
Take all of my all and all that I'll be.
I only need you to be in love with me.

Pieces of a Reluctant Memoir

Numbers and Situations

I'm taking over tragically
All the things that come undone.
Only seeing stars and stripes;
It keeps me moving on.
I haven't grown the way I should
I run around the neighborhood.
Shouting like a child through the streets
Becoming the turf that has suffered defeat.
Why is there ache in the air?
I'm feeling surrounded by weightless doubt
That pulls strings out of my hair.
Why isn't there time to see things through?
To get on with it, to mature with you.
One day I will wake and find
That I've been sucking down turpentine.
Just enough to keep me silent
But not enough to make me leave.
If there was enough in the cabinet
I'd let you in on this secret too:

I feel like I have to come unraveled
So that I can be wound back up by you.
I have to wipe my hands clean
So that I can start to feel renewed.
I'm constantly drawing straws with life
And always getting screwed.
Now that I've let go of the past
I can see how much I grew.
I only need to be inside your head
When you give me permission to.
Because I'm only human in the end;
There's not much about that I can do.

The Love

I only want you, and you know that it's true.
I only want you.
I only want you.

Pieces of a Reluctant Memoir

Part Two: The Break

Fluent in foolish
  Gathered on Sundays
Brought to you by: Hope
To be squandered on Monday.
Friendless and nameless, faceless,
Face this:
The cold air and sharp pines-
A place to be shameless.
You can have the whole week
And you still won't be blameless.

Pieces of a Reluctant Memoir

Superficial Bookmarks

The sun shines through the curtain
and I sit and kiss your shadow.
The carpet is soft like your skin
and the faintest outline of your hand
is on the cool, egg-white wall.
I try to grab it and hold it in mine
but I break nails against its surface
from my scratching and my clawing.
I get chills in your silhouette.
I'm lost in this eclipse of your love.
Your looming doppelganger sways
and I am engulfed in the darkness.

The Break

It May Be Used

If only I was a fool to believe
That everything is a mystery
And that what doesn't make sense
Makes perfectly good sense
And that's the way it's supposed to be.

Well I've been a fool for too long…
I've been devising a scheme
That will take what I mean
And turn it around til I'm wrong.
What a pretty dark and twisted dream.
If only the fools could forget all the rules
Be one with each other and
Forgive one another.
It's all about love. Isn't that good enough?
Do you need something else to believe?

Look Up At Your World

My heart
Is drenched in red wine.
It lies bare on the table
Marinating.
How it longs for your heat.
For your touch.
My heart
Knows nothing is fine.
It will simmer for hours
Contemplating.
How it will end.
How much it will hurt.
My heart
Is ready to be primed.
By your wringing out and
Grating.
So when will you stop by
And deliver me?

The Break

Hopes and Dreams Begin and End Here

Well I've been secretly crying
Over things that are out of my hands
And I feel like I'm slowly dying
In this world of reprimand.
We're fighting but we're only losing.
The odds against us are far too great.
The love we have we've been abusing
And the word Love we desecrate.
I'm not sure what that means anymore.
It's like you've already moved on.
There's no reason for you to start a war
So your side has already withdrawn.

This battle for happiness, I can't do alone.
You're the only thing on my mind.
You are the truest love I've known
And the only one I'll ever find.
Please don't leave me stranded.
You said you would never leave.
I feel like my heart has been branded.
I don't know what else to believe.
I'm trying so hard to keep my head straight
While trying harder not to surrender,
To this injustice that is far too great
Against my heart, the great defender.
But I'm not giving up on you, Dear.
Happiness is too important to lose.
Stay with me and love will adhere
If that's what you should choose.

Pieces of a Reluctant Memoir

Shoot

I'm reaching out for rapture
But I fail from living shamelessly.
I'm taken away by thoughts and presumptions
That I wish to forget and wander aimlessly.
I don't want to be your weight;
There would be no point in dragging you down.
I can't begin to sculpt decisions.
I wasn't meant to wear that evening gown.

Sunsets whisper of our embraces;
In the morning, we speak only of light.
Let's put it all behind us and begin again.
We can afford just another night.
Slander is for when we can't think of love
And passion is for when I see your face.
I was caught in a web of victorious deception,
Then devoured within your embrace.

The Break

Better than Before

I have to lift my heart up
When time drags it down.
I've been painting my eyelids
From the inside out.
Release me. Set me free. Let me
Sail away indefinitely.
I cannot embrace unwanted change.
Eventually there will be nothing for me.

I cling to frosty windows,
But when I whisper my secrets
It always fogs my vision.
And I don't know why I feel so numb-
Fingers froze, head in smoke,
I can't let go and
Pull myself free: melted and obsolete.
I don't wish for love, I say,
Let's be company.

Call Me Crazy

There isn't any sense in the things I do.
I laugh at the scenery as it changes.
I am empirical but I have no substance.
I find it convenient that I'm only convenient
When it's sleeveless nights and magazines
And collectors on the answering machine.
It's nothing but distance and hate and you.
I plan on losing until I'm at a loss.
Spend my time ignoring your existence.
Finding it harder than I would have imagined.
Odd, my imagination usually runs on overdrive
And it's no longer enduring to trust all that is behind us.
While ahead lies a carnival
Of imperfect proportions.

Part Three: The Fall

She spent the day reflecting
The way a good water-creature should.
She went through deep trenches
In the oceans of her mind
But before she could explore
What she was in there looking for
She fell into her own depression.

Mischievous Misgivings

Mischievous misgivings
They muse and they muddle
My mindful meditations
Where the makers may huddle.

At last they look longingly
Leading lost letters, the liars,
Til I'm left feeling listless
And alone in the mires.

What was wasn't wishful
But it wavered without
Though the warning it wielded
Was weaved within it, no doubt.

And I couldn't quite capture
The cold, careless cries
Of the creatures I crafted
Among cruel cumulus skies.

The Fall

Store This Soul in a Cool Dry Place

It's the story of "Mark my words."
The pen and ink shy away in the corner
While the clock on the wall
Has to ask the bird inside what time it is.
He can't seem to feel the way he used to
And the bird says he doesn't care.
We've been watching from the couch for hours.
Only I know where we've been
And what roads we've taken to get here and
You've kept track of the day, the month, the hour.
Even if the piano could play for itself
It wouldn't pay for itself.
(While the light in the hallway racks up the bills)
The police will come and drag me away
From the dishes and the laundry.
You will be frying chicken when the door
Bursts down and the sergeant trips
On the heinous wires I left cluttered for distraction.

What a story the bird will have.
He'll know of the time when I got dragged by my hair
Into the rain, with the telephone clutched in my hand-
Soap suds on my arms and face.
Anyone who knows me will forget to know me.
Everyone will focus on that damn clock in the background
And how it still doesn't have the right time.
Maybe if they opened it up from the inside they'd see
The cuckoo smoking weed and looking faded.
Maybe when the police open up the front door they'll see
The exact same thing with me.

Pieces of a Reluctant Memoir

Swaying Elegantly In My Seat

Take a good look...
I guess we'll never know
If the blood on the linoleum
Is fresh or if we haven't understood
The way it's creases like to seep
Into the bathroom or onto the carpet.
I don't know about you
But it's like I can't get anything right.
Maybe one of us will take a mop or a sponge-
Erase the path of red across the house.
My blistered feet have shown no mercy.
They work and they scrape and they breathe.
They've survived a thousand obstacles
But now I'm tethered to myself and
My razorblade has become my companion.
(We had fought for a while
And now his cut is so deep that I deserve it).
There is nothing left for him to destroy
Except for more of me.
Oh, how he slices my hands and my ears.
He watches me on my knees
Cleaning the smell of money from the floor.
Take a good look...
I guess we'll never know
If the blood on the linoleum
Is fresh.
Maybe we don't understand the way
Its creases like to seep.

The Fall

Miles Left Sleeping

I'm in a realm where nothing is real.
I've taken to drawing trees
As bare as I feel.
To the edge of the paper, but what for?
The branches seem endless;
Like me they need more.
If I were as calm as I look, believe,
The sap from the tree
Is its own way to grieve.
But I shall draw no perched birds.
There will be no caption
For I have no words.
Only thoughts of you run through my head
And the tree that I've created
And the fact that it is dead.

Ready, Set, Gone

Whatever I have written
That has offended
Has adored
Is nothing but some fruitcake
Upside down and on the floor.

Whatever I have spoken
With its flavor
After-taste
Is nothing but that fruitcake
That is ruined,
That is waste.

Whatever I have done
To make you drop it,
Make you flee
Is nothing but old fruitcake,
Simple fruitcake,
Simple me.

The Fall

Reduce, Reuse, Recycle

My brain is a giant wormhole
Amongst the fruit that is my soul.
True, I am rotten at the core,
But there's still flesh enough to eat.

Bruised and ugly, wont to evade-
Leave me among the scattered decay
Underneath the tree I fell from.
At least then will my breakdown
Serve the world its purpose.

Something Small

A demon sits upon my chest
Breathing fire in my lungs.
He bears the weight of heavy.
He speaks in many tongues.

His message is universal,
Such a powerful, tiny seed
Chanting, "You're a burden and
Death is what you need."

I fight but it's a struggle
With every weapon that I try
But he's always there regardless
For he's much stronger than I.

The longer he sits, he feasts,
Upon my thoughts, my soul, my heart
And eventually he'll consume me
For which we'll both depart.

Part Four: The Search

One side can't be defined
The other is stenciled in.
One cannot see the divide
The other sees only the end.

Incessant Gardening

Trying to find the deepness
The worth
The light within my own leaves
My place on Earth.
Falling
Diving
Falling again-
Hit the water, learn to swim.
The struggle
The split
The inner beast within.
I grow towards the light
Regardless how dim.
Fighting and clawing
Still clinging with fear.
Forfeiture is easy
Just like staying here.
My roots
My veins
Stretched like webbing
Strong like grain.
The infinite depth
The ache in my heart
It's constantly feeling
Why can't we restart?
Following seasons into years
Until I'm no longer yearning
Brain reeling, heart burning.
Left to dig alone
In dry soil at sunset.

The Search

Life's Lament

I am fake
I am false
I'm stuck in an existential loop.
Stuff me
Fluff me
I'm merely made of pipe dreams.

I cannot find my place.
I keep looking
I keep hoping
I'm starting to fall apart waiting
For a reason or a purpose.

And everything hurts
Hurts my soul
Hurt's my brain
I only feel pain.
What the hell is this place?

I saw my future ghost.
She looked inside me-
Frightened me.
Her half-smile hanging
Free but still without answers.

Pieces of a Reluctant Memoir

"He" is a Pronoun-It Replaces What's Real

Don't look to me for certainty.
I am an escape artist.
(I don't exist)
Compared to fervorless beings
I am still aware
That taking back my questions
Means never breathing air.
Whatever it was that was true
Never was
And the places they place you
Seem to engulf the real view.
Be patient with those wings!
I'm changing the scene
So that we can be free.
Not "free" as in "freedom"
But free from our beings!
No more of this acting.
No more overreacting.
No, I don't know anything
For nothing is absolute.
I am an escapist.
(Society: my rapist)
And I'm trying to find the best route
So that we could be this-
You, a prophet
And I, a muse
And we don't exist.

The Search

Pretty and Predictable

Can your starlight blossom, Supernova?
Can you wrap your heart around eternity?
Can you feel the sun and really feel it?
I know the Earth because I feel her
But I can only see the sky.
My eyes are just a product of my being
What else could I be seeing?
I only trust the things I feel.
Nothing else is as close as it seems.
Nothing else is quite as real.

Pieces of a Reluctant Memoir

A call-out to the wide-eyed, curious, inventive child:

I saw you sleeping under that large apple tree,
with a ladybug taking up residence on your smooth cheek.
The brilliant rays of light uncovering shades of blonde
in your soft, French-braided hair.
Your swimsuit faded from hours of exposure to chlorine.

I would fall in love with you, Earth child:
Your marshmallow breath and sticky fingers,
your stories, your drawings, your new contraptions,
your smile-missing teeth and all.

I watch you from the window; the rise and fall of your chest-
Evidence you are dreaming-
makes me desperate to be you:
Blowing dandelion fuzz across the yard,
saving worms from the street after the summer rain,
running over bubbles of hot tar on your bike.

Sweet, innovative, vivacious girl-
Bangs cut straight across your forehead,
dolls rested in a hammock in the corner of your room,
ideas so erratic and eccentric and essential to life.
I want to keep you locked away in my heart, my mind, my soul.
The tan moist skin tattooed with mosquito bites
The calluses on your feet from misshapen gravel,
The handprint you left mistakenly on the hallway wall.

Sleeping cherub with shadows of leaves upon your legs,
Tiny hands holding secret you've forgotten to share:
Two cerulean flowers clasped between fingers

The Search

With nails full of dirt and full of pride.
They'll be wilted by the time your light brown eyes
Open wearily to the warmth of the sunlight upon them.

Please don't ever disappear, beautiful child.
Always singing off-key to songs you don't even know,
Making tuna sandwiches for invisible friends,
Picking raspberries and throwing out the ones
With the little black bugs dwelling in the middle.

I've seen what the future holds for you;
Days where the world isn't as innocent as you.
Days where I wish you wouldn't have woken up
From under that gaping tree.
It's a shame you will have to grow up at all.
Especially since it is I who you will become.

Pieces of a Reluctant Memoir

Solitude

I am from a dangerous place
Where the veil of peace wears thin.
I was made with an irrelevant face
And was hollowed out from within.

My worth, like yours, is self-inflicted.
I have no heart, but a chest full of lies.
Love bears no weight with indictions.
The only value I have is surmised.

And that place is a desolate cavern
Filled with disease and resentful neglect.
It's cold and it smells like a tavern.
A liable home that's too broke to protect.

So I keep travelling North and stay distant
From reality, myself, and that place,
With a mask for every person in an instant
All thanks to my irrelevant face.

The Search

Unusual Donation

Without the chance of circumstance
The world is torn in half;
Those of us who wish to dream
Of universal expanse
Are set against those who need
Some spiritual assistance.

How I'd love to stop this madness;
Become a united entity
Believing only in existence.
There's much more to life than sacrifice.
Take this as my assurance:
The less time spent in apprehension
The more you'll feel its obsolescence

Uncertainty shouldn't cause deterrence.
It should be the purpose.

Part Five: The Light

There I was alone
  Falling down in a hole
A spiral against me reeling
Unsure of all feelings
Never noticing the vine
Holding on and loving mine.

Tread Lightly

I am not of the canyon
But can appreciate the beauty.
The colors, the endurance,
What's left standing when the river's gone.

I am of the river.
I am of water and life.
I fill the void, consuming,
Need to keep moving.
Stagnancy will waste me.
(Go ahead and taste me)

Holy and cleansing.
Replenishing.
The inevitably essential gift
With its burden:
To care for-to carry-whatever comes through,
Filtered and misused.

And I, this fluvial being,
Dependent as ever on something not forever,
Can only hold on through sweeping currents.

The Light

Walk With an Umbrella
(For He May Cry Above You)

Life is like wine,
So bitter to some and yet
Still tasteful to others.
It tends to come in many varieties
And the older we become the more
We value ourselves
And still...

I want to play "Mother, May I?"
With life for a while.
I want to be the one to decide
How far life can go.
I want life to take three baby steps towards me
So I can make my choices clearly.
It tends to go by so fast-
I want to stop it,
Make it go backwards;
I want life to ask me what it can and cannot do.

One day I was pretending
To be a grocer or a cook
And the next, I was that person.
I spent so many years wishing I was older
And now that time is gaining on me, I fear it.
I cower in the corner,
Shudder at words like work and bills.
My body grows older but the
Frightened child in my mind refuses to.

Pieces of a Reluctant Memoir

Life is like wine.
At some point or another
You will be forced to drink it.
The day will come when
You no longer have a choice
Of the kind you want.
We've been sipping it at church,
Sneaking it at parties,
Sometimes having to guzzle it down all at once.
And we all live not knowing when
We will taste that last pungent drop.

The Light

Breath Taking

Diving deeper into acceptance
I find nothing but the light that bursts
And absorbs my heavy heart.
It's a start.
For the first time in years, I'm craving satisfaction
From feelings, from myself-
Free the feelings, free thyself.
I am letting you out, you untamed spirit.
Crying from the hole you've been buried in
Thousands of tears ago.
In need of a resurrection,
I reach for illumination.
Digging deeper into conviction
Is the solace of my vocation.

Pieces of a Reluctant Memoir

Between the Lines

My mind has lots of beautiful thoughts
And a need to put them on paper.
I cling to the words, tiny records,
Exclusively designed by the maker.

I flower with the power it gives
When consciousness is a burden
Staking a claim, printing my name
How else do I define my person?

The Light

Hollow Stranger

Be there:
When sulking moons hang below my head
They splinter off in devious ways.
Yes, I see them shyly smile
But I'm always hanging upside down
And to me, it frowns in distaste.
Expelling its little light.
What better is it than the stars it favors?
Peeling them down from their canopy.
Beauty in the coolness; beauty in the death
Of night. For it soon brings morning.
And we are rejuvenated.
We are sanctified.

Be there:
When the fresh new day is full of ample youth.
The sun, it splinters in glorious rays.
I cannot see for it blinds my eyes
And when I'm hanging upside down-
Eyes shut, but O! It's still bright!
Covered only by thin clouds, so sporadic,
Becoming the object of my night's dreams.
Beauty in the heat and beauty in its death.
When we are sulking in the wake of night
I want to feel the light.

Sangria

I sat outside and smoked a little-
Watched the water drip from the awning above.
The morning was fresh like the dew on the grass
So I picked a stem full of wet flowers.
(They stayed by my side for company.)
I think my mind's as twisted as shrubbery
And life is more like my puffs of smoke.
Each one I expel is fast and full
But they dissipate in wisps and fade away.

There is so much life around, I'm never lonely.
Just me and my flowers, my cigarettes,
The rain from yesterday creating a miniature
Waterfall of rhythm.
The songbirds in the pines use the filters
From the ground to build a home near me.
If only everyone could feel the morning
The way that I do.

Sing, my beautiful whistler.
You have an audience in me.

Meditation

When I close my eyes
I am floating outside,
Drifting to a land filled with trees.
There's a creek that runs through
To bare fields that once grew.
Leaves dance in the autumnal breeze.
There's a house up ahead
Filled with books left unread;
Children are laughing and playing.
The goldenrods are blooming,
Earth provides the consuming.
A soft voice says, "Aren't you staying?"
But I cannot reply
So I keep drifting by
Towards the woods, I go forth again.
Traveling far past the stream,
Where I entered my dream,
All in a moment of zen.

About the Author

From a very young age Michelle Golden has held a talent and passion for writing. She considers poetry to be her most natural form of expression and an essential means for self-therapy. She has spent many years practicing and accumulating a diverse anthology of work. She spends her days balancing writing while being a stay-at-home mom to her three amazing kids. She currently resides in Wisconsin with her family.

www.ingramcontent.com/pod-product-compliance
Lightning Source LLC
Chambersburg PA
CBHW022000290426
44108CB00012B/1152